I'd rather get a spanking than go to the doctor

Written and Illustrated

by

Karen G. Frandsen

CHILDRENS PRESS ®

CHICAGO

Library of Congress Cataloging-in-Publication Data

Frandsen, Karen G.
    I'd rather get a spanking than go to the doctor.

    Summary: A child names all the urgent things that
need to be done before going to the doctor for a shot,
such as brushing teeth, doing homework, and taking
cookies to a sick friend in Alaska.
    [1. Excuses—Fiction. 2. Physicians—Fiction.
3. Medical care—Fiction] I. Title.
PZ7.F8488Id 1987   [E]   86-11735
ISBN O-516-O3498-7

Childrens Press, Chicago
Copyright ©1987 by Regensteiner Publishing Enterprises, Inc.
All rights reserved. Published simultaneously in Canada.
Printed in the United States of America.
    2 3 4 5 6 7 8 9 1O R 96 95 94 93 92 91 9O 89 88

My Mom says I have to go
to the doctor to get shots.

I say, "Not today, Mom.
I am too busy."

I go into my room to get busy. My Mom follows me. She says I have to go today.

"But I don't need shots," I say.

I go outside to jump rope.

My Mom follows me. She says I might get very sick if I don't have shots.

I already feel sick. I go
to my room to lie down.
I close my eyes and try
to rest.

My Mom follows me. She says I can rest when I get home.

I say, "OK.

"But, first I better clean my room. Then, I have to brush my teeth, feed my dog, do my homework, and take some cookies to my sick friend who lives far away."

I get up to get cookies.

My Mom is standing in the doorway. She is not smiling.

I start to cry.

My Mom hugs me. She says to wash my face and I will feel better.

I say, "Not going to the doctor will make me feel better. An ice cream will make me feel better.

"Even getting a spanking
will make me feel better
than going to the doctor."

My Mom says, "Even a spanking?"
Well, maybe not a spanking.

I get into the car. We drive to the doctor's office.

I am still crying.

The doctor says, "Hi."

He says I am getting big.
I think I am too big to get
shots. Maybe I am too big
to go to the doctor.

Just as I get up to
leave, the doctor rolls up
my sleeve. He has a needle
in his hand.

I scream very loud.

The doctor says, "Why
are you screaming? I didn't
give you a shot yet."

He asks me if I can
count all the balloons on
the wall. I start to count.

Then he says, "All done.
That wasn't so bad, was it?"

My Mom says, "Don't you feel better?"
I say, "An ice cream would make me feel better."

My Mom says, "Don't you
want to clean your room
first, brush your teeth,
feed your dog, do your
homework, and take some
cookies to your sick friend
who lives far away?"

Maybe my friend shouldn't have cookies when he is sick. Maybe he should have shots, too.

I feel better now. But,
I'd still like an ice cream.

About the author/artist

Karen Frandsen grew up in southern California and presently lives in San Diego with her children, Eric and Ingrid.

Ms. Frandsen is a free-lance artist and elementary school teacher. This is the third book she has written and illustrated for Childrens Press.

The real experiences of her two children and her students are the basis for her books.